Stuck Between A Rock And A Hard Place

KINSHUK CHAKRABORTY

Made with ❤ on the BookLeaf Publishing Platform
www.bookleafpub.in
www.bookleafpub.com

Dedication

To Nana, who still wakes my soul every morning with memories of her gentle footsteps at dawn.

Preface

In writing these poems, I found myself mapping the territory between aspiration and reality, between the dreams we nurture and the lives we actually lead. These verses emerged from late-night commutes, fluorescent-lit offices, and quiet moments of reflection - spaces where our carefully constructed plans collide with life's unyielding circumstances. They chronicle the peculiar experience of a generation caught between traditional expectations and modern ambitions, between Instagram-worthy success stories and the mundane reality of paying bills. Some were written on coffee-stained napkins during lunch breaks, others typed hastily on my phone while pretending to take meeting notes. Together, they form a topography of compromise, resilience, and unexpected beauty found in the spaces we never planned to inhabit.

Acknowledgements

I am forever indebted to my family, who cultivated my love for literature by surrounding me with books in Bengali, English, etc., showing me how emotions could dance differently across languages. To Sukumar Ray, whose *Abol Tabol* opened my eyes to the magic of wordplay and taught me that poetry could live in the delightful space between profound and playful—your influence runs through every verse I write. And finally, to BookLeaf Publishing, who saw potential in these midnight musings and margin scribbles, transforming my private reflections into shared experiences—thank you for giving these words a home beyond my notebooks.

THE WEIGHT OF WORDS

Each morning as I face the empty page,
I feel the pressure of ten thousand books
Already written, stacked in dusty rows
Or floating weightless in the digital
Expanse that spans our modern consciousness.
What wisdom can I add that hasn't been
Expressed in better words by keener minds?
The libraries of Alexandria
Now fit inside a pocket, yet we scroll
Past genius without pause or reverence,
Our thumbs conducting symphonies of thought
Into oblivion with casual swipes.

My mind, once sharp as winter morning frost,
Now struggles holding memories in place.
They slip between the cracks of countless tabs,
Dispersed across the servers' endless reach.
Why memorize when search engines can fetch
Any fact within a microsecond's breath?
Yet something's lost in this efficiency—
The slow digestion of a hard-won truth,
The mental paths we forge through wilderness
Of thought, the satisfaction of recall.

Still, here I am, attempting once again
To carve new channels through familiar stone,
To find fresh water in a well-drunk stream.
Perhaps the value lies not in the words
Themselves, but in the act of seeking them—
Each generation's need to speak anew
Their ancient truths in modern dialect,
To feel the weight of wisdom in their hands
And pass it on, transformed but undiminished,
Into the ever-growing sea of thought.

TRAVEL TROUBLES

3

At home, my feet itch with mapped-out dreams,
each ceiling fan blade points to a different continent,
while my coffee mug collects imaginary passport stamps.
But in Arunachal, I miss the specific creak of my
bedroom floor,
in Pune, I long for my grandmother's cooking,
in Shillong, the call to prayer reminds me of my mother's
voice.
My heart is a compass that always points homeward
except when I'm home—then it spins wild with
wanderlust,
like a bird that builds its nest with foreign feathers
but weeps for its first tree when flying south.
Home is everywhere I'm not, and nowhere I am.

FOR A FEW FRAMES TOGETHER

I want to sit beside you in the dark,
not touching, but close enough
to hear your breath catch
when the ghost appears,
or the joke lands,
or the king makes his fatal move.

I want to watch your face
in the flickering light,
as *Munjya*'s absurdity breaks
across your features like dawn,
your laughter becoming
the better half of mine.

I want to see *Ludo*'s threads
weave through your mind,
catch the subtle shift
in your posture when you
piece together the puzzle
before I do, or after—
either way, a delight.

I want to share silence

when Mirza and Meer
contemplate their chess pieces,
while empire crumbles
around their ivory towers.
To exchange glances that say
"See how blind we too can be
to the world burning beyond
our precious games?"

I want to build a fortress
of borrowed moments,
where our shadows merge
on the screen between scenes,
where we can trade whispers
like contraband:
"Watch this part—"
"Did you catch that—"
"Oh god, here it comes—"

I want to split samosas
during intermission,
dropping crumbs like breadcrumbs
to find our way back
to this accidental intimacy,
this borrowed belonging.

Let us be strangers

who know each other
perfectly for three hours,
who understand without words
why that scene made us both
lean forward in our seats,
why that dialogue drew
matching sighs from our lips.

When the credits roll,
we'll gather our things,
step back into our separate stories.
But for now, in this darkness,
let us be fellow travellers,
cosmic debris drawn briefly
into the same orbit,
sharing the same gravity
of plot and emotion,
breathing the same suspense,
tasting the same catharsis.

For just these few frames,
let us be one audience,
one consciousness,
one heart beating
in time with the film's pulse—
then release me
to my solitude,

knowing somewhere
you carry the same scenes,
the same moments,
like secret constellations
we once mapped together
in the dark.

KITCHEN CATASTROPHES

I thought I'd master Bengali fare,
My dreams filled with fragrant rice and dal,
But every attempt led to a fall—
The kitchen filled with black despair.

The rice turned mushy, thick as glue,
While dal became a concrete mass;
Each spoonful made my family pass,
Their faces wearing shades of blue.

The fish I tried to gently fry
Disintegrated in the pan;
From fish to mush—my masterplan
Made grandmas cry.

The chicken curry brought such shame,
Too tough to pierce with sharpest knife;
My mother, bless her patient life,
Just smiled and took the blame.

But eggs! Oh eggs became my friend,
The one thing I could safely make;
No matter if I'd burn or break
All else from start to end.

So now when asked about my skill,
I proudly boast of perfect eggs,
While quietly, on bended legs,
I practice cooking still.

For one day soon, I swear it's true,
My rice will fluff, my dal will shine,
My fish and chicken will divine—
Till then, omelettes will do!

A GOURMAND'S CONFESSIONS

Light biryani, they say—
but I laugh at the oxymoron
because who counts calories
when there's joy swimming
in pools of ghee and love?

During quarantine,
vada pav became my religion:
that spicy potato heart,
those green chutney prayers,
delivered by masked prophets
on scooters through empty streets.

Peanuts rattle in my backpack
like tiny maracas of joy,
my travel companions
through dust and distance,
through cities and stories—
shell fragments marking my trail
like breadcrumbs in a fairy tale.

At 3 AM, my soda cans
hiss secrets to my textbooks,

bubbles rising like solutions
to my research questions,
caffeine dancing with
citations in my head.

Mom's noodles don't know
they're supposed to be straight—
they curl like questions,
twist like her smile when she says
"Just one more bowl?"
(There's always one more bowl.)

Lunch break dosas arrive
like crispy sun disks,
their edges collecting minutes
I should spend working,
but who can type with
sambar-dipped fingers?

Dad appears with roshogollas
like a magician pulling sweets
from grocery bag hats—
"Just happened to pass the shop,"
he lies, and I pretend
I haven't seen the receipt
falling from his pocket.

And oh, the namkeens!
Hidden in kitchen corners
like guilty little treasures—
my midnight fingers know
their jar-top choreography,
the silent twist and dip
while everyone sleeps.
(But why are they always
half-empty when mom checks?
Surely the house ghosts
must love them too.)

My love story is measured
in empty plates and full hearts,
in the way food finds me
when I'm not even looking,
in the cheese pulls of life,
in the crunch of memories,
in the taste of now,
and the hunger for what's next.

Just don't ask me about diets—
my taste buds are allergic
to the word "no"
and my heart beats
in flavours, not numbers.

ON THE POST-STRUCTURAL PARADIGMS OF NOTHING IN PARTICULAR

In consideration of the dialectical praxis
Of hermeneutical taxonomies vis-à-vis
The socio-cultural matrix of cheese,
I hereby propose my thesis.

Through dense theoretical frameworks that float
Like untethered signifiers around a footnote,
I deconstruct the liminal spaces between
What I meant to say and what I wrote.

My methodology, rigorously vague,
Employs qualitative analysis so plague-
-iarized from theorists long deceased,
Their ghosts demand a footnote league.

The literature review reveals a gap
So vast it might just be a nap
Between two thousand cited works
That no one ever read, perhaps.

My contribution to the field
(If such epistemic fruits should yield)
Lies somewhere in the intersection
Of what seven reviewers failed to shield.

Through careful application of Foucault,
(Though what he means, I do not know)
I problematize the very notion
Of having anywhere to go.

In conclusion, though inconclusive,
My findings prove somewhat elusive,
Suggesting further research needs
Funding that's far more inclusive.

Bibliography stretching miles,
Archived in taxonomic files,
Citations breeding citations
In proper academic styles.

THE DAILY ODYSSEY

When dawn breaks softly on my window's frosted pane,
I rise before the world has stirred from slumber deep.
My journey calls, a promise I must daily keep—
Through winding roads and paths that time has made
mundane.

At six, I join the weary travellers' solemn queue,
Some choose the bus, while others crowd in shared cab
seats.
The sumo growls through morning's fog and empty
streets,
As stories of our lives blend with the morning dew.

Two hours pass like leaves swept up in autumn's dance,
The city greets me with its chaos, smoke, and sound.
My colleagues wait, their bikes and cars all rally-bound,
Through traffic's maze we weave, caught in a daily
trance.

Sometimes I chart a different course through time and
space,
Departing later, landing in a halfway town.
An auto rickshaw bears me up and sets me down
Where village roads embrace the morning's gentler

grace.

A friend awaits upon his trusty scooter there,
Two wheels become our chariot through dusty roads.
We share the weight of morning's heavy, silent loads,
As wind and speed dissolve the day's persistent care.

Six hours each day—a pilgrimage of sorts, I guess,
Through seasons' change and weather's wild, untamed
moods.
In monsoon rains or summer's scorching interludes,
The journey molds my hours with its firm caress.

These roads have watched me laugh and curse and
sometimes weep,
They've heard my dreams whispered at breaking light of
day.
They've seen me race when time slips treacherously
away,
And felt my tired footsteps when my pace turns deep.

The vehicles change like actors in some cosmic play,
While I remain, the constant in this shifting scene.
Through dust and din, through landscapes gold and grey
and green,
I trace these paths that have become my second way.

My life is measured now in miles and minutes passed,
In faces glimpsed through windows steamed with
morning's breath,
In stories shared with strangers till our paths diverge,
In hopes that someday, somewhere, peace will come at
last.

Yet humour finds me in this daily marathon—
The sumo driver's jokes, the auto's wild swerve,
My colleague's tales that help our weary spirits serve
The distance yet to cover before day is gone.

The roads have taught me patience, shown me grace and
grit,
Three hours out, three hours back—a lifetime spent
In motion, caught between the gone and yet-to-be,
While somewhere in between, I've learned to make it fit.

HOLIDAY PARADOX: A SESTINA

I planned a perfect day, just for me,
No work—just games and Bhaduri's stories.
First, booting up my game controller,
Loading *AC: Valhalla* in its brutal glory,
Each quest and fight giving me a chill,
Yet somehow leading to exhaustion.

I didn't expect this swift exhaustion,
As these pastimes drain energy from me.
Reading horror should give a pleasant chill,
But I rush through all of Bhaduri's stories,
Chasing each achievement's hollow glory,
My thumb aching on the controller.

Hour six gripping tight the controller,
Eyes burning with screen exhaustion,
Each completed quest less filled with glory.
The rhythm starts to irritate me—
I force myself through horror stories,
No longer feeling any real chill.

What started as excitement's chill
Now feels forced. The game controller

Sits heavy as I switch to stories,
But reading breeds its own exhaustion.
These choices now constrain me,
Stripped of their intended glory.

I sought too hard to grasp the glory
Of gaming's adrenaline chill,
Of words that used to calm me.
Now both the book and controller
Feed into growing exhaustion,
As I push through games and stories.

I can't stop checking off these stories,
Each ending's diminishing glory.
My brain screams with exhaustion,
Body tense with anxious chill.
I still clutch the controller,
These hobbies now controlling me.

My stories lost their glory, left just chill;
The controller breeds pure exhaustion,
As leisure time overwhelms me.

4 AM

It's 4 AM again
and I'm still awake,
screen glowing in darkness
like I used to be, years ago.

Back then, I'd hear my grandmother's footsteps,
precise and purposeful at dawn—
her day beginning as mine refused to end.
She'd open my door, checking,
and I'd quickly shut my eyes,
breathing slow, measured, fake.

Sometimes she caught me,
my screen betraying my act,
her voice stern but soft:
"Still awake? Don't you know what time it is?"
I'd smile, guilty, caught.

Sometimes I'd ask her
"Wake me at seven?"
And she always would,
gentle hands shaking me awake,
never failing, never late.

Years passed, roles reversed—
I'd wake early for work,
peek into her room,
"I'm leaving, Nana"
Her tired eyes opening briefly,
a weak smile, a whispered "Take care."

Now my alarm rings at dawn,
but her footsteps don't follow.
No one checks if I'm still awake,
no one to pretend-sleep for,
no one to wake me,
no one to tell "I'm leaving."

Some mornings I still wake at 4,
sitting in darkness,
waiting for footsteps that won't come.
I want her to catch me again,
scold me for staying up,
just one more time.

Her photograph watches
from my bedside table
as I count hours till dawn,
my nocturnal habits unchanged,
but the house stays silent now
at 4 AM.

THE WEIGHT OF TWENTY RUPEES

Winter morning, the air sharp as broken glass—
there she stood, wrapped in a dark shawl
that seemed to absorb what little warmth
the January sun could spare.

Her white sari, threadbare as morning mist,
barely covered feet that had forgotten
the comfort of shoes. Time had carved
valleys into her cheeks, where shadows pooled
like collected sorrows.

Our eyes met across the waiting space,
her palm extended like a bridge
between two worlds. Not begging,
no—there was something else
in those eyes, clouded with age
but bright with untold stories.

I saw her, and yet didn't see her,
my mind already racing ahead
to meetings and deadlines,
the day's choreography of importance
that now seems so hollow.

Twenty rupees—a gesture so small
it shames me still. There in my pocket,
a hundred waited, heavy with possibility,
while my heart played miser
with paper-thin excuses.

"Babu," she called after me,
her voice carrying the weight
of a thousand grandmothers,
each syllable a soft rebuke
to my hurrying soul.

The word follows me still,
echoes in empty moments,
that tender address that held
neither judgment nor blame,
just a gentle reaching out
across the chasm of generations.

What stories died unspoken
that morning? What wisdom
went unshared, what blessings
ungiven, as I chose
the sterile comfort
of being on time?

I search for her now,
in every white sari
that floats past my vision,
in every elderly face
that turns my way.
But winter has given way
to spring, to summer,
to monsoon, to winter again,
and she remains
a ghost of grace denied.

The twenty rupees sits
like a stone in my memory,
not for its meagre sum,
but for the lesson it taught:
how poverty lives not just
in empty pockets
but in hearts too full
of their own importance
to stop, to listen,
to simply be human
for one precious moment.

I carry her "Babu" like a mantra,
a reminder that time is not always
currency to be spent,
but sometimes a gift

to be given freely,
even to strangers
who might have been,
for one sacred moment,
grandmother, teacher, guide—
had I only stayed
to listen.

KHICHDI AND REVELATIONS

Steam rises from the massive pot like incense,
prayers whispered between stirring ladles
and hands passing steel plates in assembly lines.
The kitchen floor sticky with spilled dal,
yellow footprints marking our dance of service.

People I barely spoke to all year
now direct traffic with authority of generals,
their dress hitched up, sleeves rolled,
calling orders across the chaos—
more ghee, more plates, more hands needed.

And they come, waves of humanity
through our gates thrown wide—
the rickshaw-wala who waves each morning,
the widow from three streets over,
the children who play cricket in our lane.
All equal before Maa Saraswati's grace,
all hungry for blessing and belonging.

The neighbour I thought too proud to visit
washes dishes without being asked,
while my friend and cousin, blood of my blood,

sends a text: "Too busy, maybe next year."
Revelations served hot with khichdi,
truth spooned out with every helping.

In this crush of bodies and bhajans,
I learn to read the heart's hidden script:
how family is not always of our choosing,
how love arrives wearing stranger's faces,
how service binds us closer than blood.

The woman who sells flowers by the temple
brings fresh marigolds for the goddess,
stays to help arrange prasad plates—
her calloused hands moving with such grace
I feel ashamed of my previous blindness.

Night falls, and still they come,
drawn by the light of lanterns and faith,
each face illuminated by something larger
than the sum of rice and lentils,
larger than the walls that usually divide us.

In the morning, I will find turmeric stains
on my best white kurta, and remember:
how the universe conspires to teach us
through the simplest of meals,
how wisdom comes ladled out

in moments we least expect,
how the heart expands
one blessing at a time,
one plate at a time,
one revelation at a time.

ODE TO THE THREADS OF MY LIFE

First came SHU in my earliest days,
A friendship brief that couldn't stay.
But JOH, younger by four years' time,
Has stayed beside me, rain or shine.

School brought AR, DE, SO, PO and RA,
Each with their own paths to display.
They needed me when times were rough,
But their own worlds were quite enough.
I chose to walk away from most,
Though RA's friendship wasn't lost.

College introduced a different crew:
AB, SH, NE, CHI, RU and DO came through.
AB and NE still stick around,
The truest friends I've ever found.

University expanded wide,
First CHI and I walked side by side.
MON and MAN joined soon enough,
Through bus rides, projects, smooth and tough.
Then GAU became my closest friend,
Two minds that seemed to comprehend

Each other's thoughts without a word,
A brotherhood that life conferred.

MANO, DEV, and SHAB deserve their space,
Always there, a steady base.
JOH remains unchanged and true,
While with AB, NE, MON and GAU,
I often feel like extra weight,
So I choose to step away and wait.

New friends have joined along the way:
At university, PRI and SAY
Have become my trusted guides.
While SU and PR share travel rides.
SAY and PRI I lean on most,
When doubts and fears leave me engrossed.

Some friends were meant for just a while,
Others stayed to share each mile.
Some drifted off, some closer grew,
Each one taught me something new.
Not every friendship's meant to last,
But each one shapes who we become at last.

OFFICE

These fluorescent lights above me cast shadows on my
screen
While I type up memos that nobody's going to read
Another meeting called at five, they know I need to leave
But I smile and nod politely, while my spirit starts to
bleed

The boss walks by my cubicle, looks down with that
same sneer
Been working here two years now, still treat me like I
just appeared
"Could you stay late tonight?" Not really a question I
hear
More like a royal decree, while my dreams just disappear

These office walls are closing in
I bite my tongue, suppress the scream
They'll never know what's deep within
This rage behind my practiced grin

Got my degree with honours, now I'm filing papers away
While they take credit for my work, what else is new
today?
"Thanks for your suggestion," then they shoot it down

anyway
Keep my thoughts locked in a vault, that's the price I got
to pay

In the break room whispers flow, politics and subtle
games
Every day I navigate through their power-tripping
games
Got my bills to pay though, so I dance within their
frames
Swallow pride with coffee grounds, these isn't even
corporate chains

Sometimes late at night I write
All the words I cannot say
Delete them all by morning light
Another role I have to play

So I sit here in my chair, watching seconds tick away
Building castles in my mind where I finally have my say
Where respect isn't just a poster hanging on the wall to
sway
Till then I'll keep on grinding, till I find a better way

SIX HEARTS

One
Now your face fills screens and billboards
While my heart remembers you smaller
Before fame claimed you
When my chest would flutter at your presence
A passing fancy, perhaps
But one that taught me how hearts can stumble

Two
You read the books I read
Spoke the words I longed to hear
Your years ahead of mine didn't matter
Until they did
When your path led elsewhere
Leaving me with dog-eared pages of what could have
been

Three
We competed for everything
Each victory a wound
Each defeat a scar
My heart raced not from affection
But from the need to win you
Strange how desire and destruction danced together

Four
I tried reshaping myself
Into the mold you sought
But your checklist had no space
For someone like me
I learned then that hearts can't bend
Into shapes they weren't meant to take

Five
We mirrored each other too well
Both hiding behind cautious smiles
Sharing train rides and careful conversations
Our shadows touching but never our hands
Two wallflowers afraid to bloom
In case the other might wilt

Six
Your brilliant mind sparked and fizzled
Like a storm I watched from far away
Too distant to get struck
Too removed to get burned
While you blazed your peculiar path
I stayed in my comfortable shade

Now
I've found peace in empty spaces

Where no heart beats but mine
No steps to match
No rhythms to follow
Just the quiet certainty
That some souls are meant to walk alone

THE PENCIL SHARPENER ON THE BUS

A plastic pencil sharpener falls onto my lap
During the evening commute home.
Small, red, unremarkable—
I don't know whose it is or how it got there.

I hold it in my palm
And suddenly I am nineteen again,
Sitting at my desk with papers spread wide,
Drawing characters with careful strokes,
Writing stories in margins of notebooks,
Dreaming of manga panels and published works.

I was going to be an artist then,
A storyteller, a creator.
My teachers called me talented,
My friends read my stories,
I won competitions and medals,
Proud scholar with endless possibilities.

Now I shuffle through excel sheets,
File papers, attend meetings,
Write emails instead of stories,
Draw pie charts instead of heroes.

The stories remain untold,
The sketches never made.

The bus jerks to a stop—my stop.
No one claims the sharpener.
I place it on the warm seat,
Stand up, straighten my office clothes,
Step out into the evening air
Carrying only my laptop bag
And the weight of abandoned dreams.

The bus drives away,
Taking with it the red sharpener
And the ghosts of what could have been.
Tomorrow I will be back at my desk,
But tonight, just for a moment,
I remembered who I wanted to be.

ON FRIENDSHIP AND FADING

I used to think that friendship was a thread
That, woven tight through careful hands and time,
Would strengthen with each passing day and bind
Us closer through the storms of growing up.
How naive that belief appears to me.

I chose my friends with careful thought, each one
A treasured presence in my measured life.
No feast of shallow bonds for me—I kept
A smaller table, set with deeper plates,
Believing quality outweighed the crowd.

But lately I have watched the ways they drift
Like leaves caught in a stream I cannot cross:
Their "maybe later" texts that never bloom
To calls, their gatherings I glimpse online
Where I, somehow, was never asked to come.

I see them meet in combinations new,
Their lives now intertwined through my design—
The introductions that I orchestrated,
Not knowing I was building bridges that
Would carry them away from where I stand.

The truth sits bitter on my tongue: I am
The backup plan, the afterthought, the friend
They text when primary plans fall through.
My calls ring hollow in their busy lives,
While theirs command my swift attendance still.

Others guard their circles jealously,
Keep friendship groups distinct as separate stars.
I thought this isolation primitive,
Not seeing how it gave them power, kept
Their relationships from slow dissolving.

I will not beg for scraps of attention,
Or plead for inclusion in their plans.
My dignity demands more than the role
Of understudy in this friendship play,
Where I seem cast in ever-shrinking parts.

My books wait patient on their shelves, my games
Stand ready for my solitary joy.
My hobbies don't require consensus or
Approval from a group too busy now
To notice when I slowly step away.

I gave respect and time in equal share,
Expected not excess but equity—

A basic balance in our give and take.
If this makes me demanding, let it be.
I'd rather stand alone than stoop to beg.

So let them drift together, let them build
Their bonds without my presence as the bridge.
I'll tend my garden of contentment here,
Where solitude bears sweeter fruit than that
Which grows from obligation's withered vine.

THE SPIDER ON THE WATER CLOSET

You've made your home where I am most exposed,
A witness to my morning rituals,
My midnight stumbles, bleary-eyed and slow.
I see your legs first—thin black exclamations
Against the porcelain's unforgiving white.

We have this dance, you and I: when I lean
Too close, you skitter to your shadow-space
Behind the bowl, where pipes meet tiled wall.
I've never named you—names would make this strange
Agreement we've developed far too real.

Some nights I sit and watch you watching me,
Your eight eyes catching light like tiny stars.
We're most ourselves in darkness, aren't we, friend?
When social graces slip away like web
Strands breaking in the morning's first fresh breeze.

I could have killed you forty times by now.
You could have crept across my sleeping face.
Instead, we've chosen this peculiar peace:
You stay just visible enough to warn
Me of your presence; I pretend you're not.

I wonder what you make of human ways—
The water's sudden roar, the paper squares,
The ritual washing of the hands, the way
I stand or sit depending on the need.
Do you judge my habits from your corner perch?

Sometimes I talk to you on harder days,
When loneliness feels thick as morning fog.
You never answer, but you never leave,
A constant in my most private moments,
Silent keeper of my whispered truths.

What do your children think of this strange beast
Who visits you so regularly here?
Do you tell stories of the giant who
Allows you tenure in this porcelain realm,
Who spares your life though he could end it quick?

We are unlikely roommates, you and I,
Sharing this space of vulnerability—
You, exposed upon your wall-side vigil,
Me, in my most unguarded human state,
Both pretending not to see the other.

Perhaps there's wisdom in this compromise,
This wordless treaty signed in glances, built

On mutual recognition of our needs:
You for a home, me for some company,
Even in life's most solitary room.

THE THING BENEATH

Beneath the bed it scratches low,
Each plank of wood a splintered feast.
Not ghost, not shadow, something least
Of all the terrors one could know.

The darkness thickens, hour by hour,
As fingernails rake wooden grain.
My sanctuary turns profane—
This room no longer my safe tower.

I cannot glimpse what lurks below,
Though shadows dance on mirrored glass.
The minutes agonizingly pass;
Its presence poisons time's sweet flow.

The light switch mocks from yards away,
Too far to reach without descent.
My muscles tight, my courage spent,
As something ancient starts to sway.

The scratching stops—a moment's peace?
But silence breeds a deeper dread.
The space beneath my waiting bed
Holds breath that will not grant release.

Perhaps if stillness claims my form,
It might forget that I am here.
But in the dark, I sense it near,
As static crackles before storm.

Tonight the scratching sounds draw blood
From timber seasoned with my fear.
Each night it climbs a fraction near;
Soon nothing will contain its flood.

Yet could these horrors simply be
The shadows of my fractured mind?
Each terror that I think I find—
Perhaps the monster here is me.

QUEST

Lo! When Aurora's fingers brush the sky,
Our valiant hero hears the clarion call
(His phone's alarm, set thrice lest courage fail),
And from his downy fortress must arise.
What epic struggle 'twixt the warmth of sheets
And duty's stern command! Like knights of old
Who donned their armour piece by heavy piece,
He garbs himself in corporate chainmail:
The sacred tie, the blessed button-down,
The polished shoes that echo tales of war.

Through treacherous realms (the station's dark domain),
Where metal dragons screech and humans press
Like armies clashing in some ancient vale,
Our hero stands, his backpack as his shield.
The office tower, like some castle grand,
Looms high above the morning's misty realm,
Its glass and steel a challenge to the brave.

Within these halls, what battles rage unseen!
What jousts of words with supervisors stern,
Who, like the dragons of an elder age,
Breathe fire through emails marked "URGENT - REPLY!"
Each meeting room's a tournament of wits,

Each deadline like a quest for holy grails,
Each PowerPoint a scroll of ancient lore.

When evening's shadows lengthen o'er the land,
Our warrior, weary from his daily strife,
Takes up his trusty bus once more.
Through rush hour's chaos, worthy of crusades,
He battles homeward, stomach's growls his spur,
Like chargers spurring knights to victory.

Yet know ye this: behind these mighty deeds,
These daily labours worthy of old songs,
There lies a truth more tender than the dawn.
For in a modest castle down the way,
Two gentle souls await their champion's tale—
His mother's smile, his father's quiet pride,
Worth more than all the kingdoms of the earth.
For them he'd storm a thousand meetings more,
Face countless deadlines, brave the darkest trains,
And count each battle won, each struggle blessed,
If but to keep that light within their eyes,
That joy that makes a warrior's heart soar high.
For love, not glory, makes the truest knight,
And home's the sweetest victory of all.

SARASWATI PUJA

In the quiet corner of my home,
White flowers and incense trace paths through morning
light,
As Maa Saraswati's presence settles like dew
On books laid carefully at her feet.

The priest's chants weave with my mother's prayers,
Sanskrit flowing like the river of knowledge
That streams from the Goddess's veena strings.
I watch, and in watching, begin to understand.

Peace is not a gift unwrapped in solitude,
But a blessing passed from hand to hand,
Like the prasad we share, sweet on the tongue,
Made sacred by the giving and receiving.

I think of the storms I've weathered,
The nights when wisdom felt distant as stars,
When my prayers seemed to echo in empty rooms—
Now I see: those were the lessons she sent.

For how can we know the weight of peace
Without having carried chaos?
How can we taste the sweetness of blessing

Without having drunk from bitter cups?

The smoke from the dhoop rises,
Carrying our offerings skyward
Like the questions I once hurled at silence,
Now returning as gentle answers.

In this moment of crystal clarity,
Between the sharp edges of then and now,
I see why we gather, why we pray:
Peace is a circle, not a line.

It flows from the Goddess to the elder's hands
From parent to child, teacher to student,
A river of grace that carries us all,
If only we learn to float.

Let this puja be more than memory,
More than tradition kept for tradition's sake.
Let it be the anchor I cast into tomorrow's storms,
The white lotus blooming in troubled waters.

For now I understand—
The blessing was always here,
In the hands that taught me to pray,
In the voices that showed me how to sing,

In the long road that led me home
To this moment of perfect peace.

PAGES

The notebook sits heavy in my hands,
decades pressed between covers.
Each leaf holds a different version of me -
the boy who believed in forever,
the man who learned otherwise.

Coffee rings mark the winter
I couldn't sleep, kept vigil
by lamplight, writing until dawn.
Tear stains blur the ink
where grief spilled over.

Some pages are crisp with certainty,
others soft from being turned
again and again, as if rereading
might change their ending.
Dog-eared corners mark the moments
I keep returning to.

The margins overflow with afterthoughts,
crossed-out lines speak louder
than the words that replaced them.
Empty spaces tell their own stories
between carefully crafted sentences.

Near the end, blank pages wait.
My hand hovers over fresh paper,
pen poised, knowing each word written
becomes permanent, even when crossed out.
Even erasures leave their mark.

I add today's entry:
the weight of the book,
the afternoon light,
of a possibility
of pages yet to come.